SUPERIOR ANIMAL SENSES

HOW
CATS
AND OTHER ANIMALS
SEE AT NIGHT

Christine Honders

Published in 2016 by The Rosen Publishing Group, Inc.
29 East 21st Street, New York, NY 10010

First Edition

Editor: Katie Kawa
Book Design: Reann Nye

Photo Credits: Cover Tetra Images - Wim van den Heever/Brand X Pictures/ Getty Images; p. 4 (domestic cat) Djomas/Shutterstock.com; p. 4 (mountain lion) mlorenz/Shutterstock.com; p. 5 Jason Prince/Shutterstock.com; p. 7 Stocktrek/ Stockbyte/Getty Images; p. 8 Gary C. Tognoni/Shutterstock.com; p. 9 (top) Nejron Photo/Shutterstock.com; p. 9 (bottom) Maciej Bledowski/Shutterstock.com; p. 11 (both) Designua/Shutterstock.com; p. 13 Per-Gunnar Ostby/Oxford Scientific/ Getty Images; p. 15 (top) O.Bellini/Shutterstock.com; p. 15 (bottom) tonfon/ Shutterstock.com; pp. 16, 17 Ryan M. Bolton/Shutterstock.com; p. 18 KOJI SASAHARA/AP Images; p. 19 Nikitin Mikhail/Shutterstock.com; p. 20 EpicStockMedia/Shutterstock.com; p. 21 Nightman1965/Shutterstock.com; p. 22 olga_gl/Shutterstock.com.

Library of Congress Cataloging-in-Publication Data

Honders, Christine.
How cats and other animals see at night / by Christine Honders.
p. cm. — (Superior animal senses)
Includes index.
ISBN 978-1-4994-0989-5 (pbk.)
ISBN 978-1-4994-1029-7 (6 pack)
ISBN 978-1-4994-1059-4 (library binding)
1. Nocturnal animals — Juvenile literature. I. Honders, Christine. II. Title.
QL755.5 H65 2016
591.5'18—d23

Manufactured in the United States of America

CPSIA Compliance Information: Batch #WS15PK: For Further Information contact Rosen Publishing, New York, New York at 1-800-237-9932

CONTENTS

NIGHT SIGHT

Have you ever wondered how cats can sneak around the house at night without knocking anything over? How can some animals live in the woods and always find their way in the dark? Some animals are awake all night long and sleep during the day!

Animals need to **adapt** to changes in the world around them in order to stay alive. Some have adapted a strong sense of smell or hearing. This book will focus on animals that can see in the dark, including many different kinds of cats—from mountain lions to house cats.

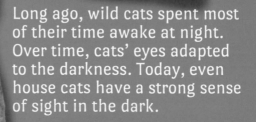

Long ago, wild cats spent most of their time awake at night. Over time, cats' eyes adapted to the darkness. Today, even house cats have a strong sense of sight in the dark.

THAT MAKES SENSE!

All cats belong to the same animal family, but they're split into two groups: big cats and small cats. Big cats, such as lions and tigers, can roar. Small cats, such as mountain lions and house cats, purr instead of roar.

LIVING IN THE DARK

People sometimes get nervous in the dark because they can't see well and don't know what's around them. For some animals, night is their time to work and play! They're at their best in the dark because of their strong senses, including night vision. Animals that are most active at night are called nocturnal animals.

Animals are nocturnal for many reasons. In very hot places, it's much cooler at night. Bats fly at night so they don't have to fight with birds to get food. It's also easier for animals to hide from predators at night.

THAT MAKES SENSE!

Some animals become nocturnal when they live close to humans. Raccoons and rabbits look for food at night so they can avoid running into people.

Mountain lions hunt at night.
They use their night vision to
help them catch **prey**.

How Big Your Eyes Are!

Cats, like many nocturnal animals, have big eyes. Their pupils open more widely than those of animals that don't see well at night. Pupils are the dark spots in the middle of the eye that let light in. Larger pupils allow more light into the eye, making it easier to see in the dark.

When a cat's pupils are at their widest, they cover almost the entire front of its eyes. Cats' eyes let in so much light that they only need about one-sixth of the light humans need in order to see.

THAT MAKES SENSE!

Owls are also known for their big eyes. Owls' eyes can't roll in their **sockets** like people's eyes do. Instead, owls turn their head almost all the way around!

8

Owls and cats have large pupils. Special **muscles** make the pupils larger or smaller to let in more or less light.

After light enters the pupil, it goes through the lens and onto the retina. The retina is the control center of the eye. It's connected to the brain. The retina has two kinds of light-sensing cells called rods and cones. Cones work in bright light, and rods are what help the eye see in low light.

Cats and other nocturnal animals have retinas with many rods and very few cones. Rods don't let eyes see colors, but cones do. Most nocturnal animals don't see color well since they don't have many cones.

THAT MAKES SENSE!

The light-sensing cells in the eye are also called photoreceptors. "Photo" means "light," and "receptor" means "receiver."

EYE CHART

ROD	CONE
WHAT DOES IT LOOK LIKE?	

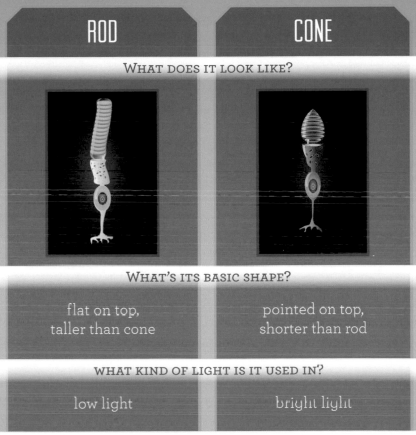

ROD	CONE
WHAT'S ITS BASIC SHAPE?	
flat on top, taller than cone	pointed on top, shorter than rod
WHAT KIND OF LIGHT IS IT USED IN?	
low light	bright light
WHAT'S IT GOOD AT SENSING?	
motion, shapes	details, color
IS IT FOUND IN A NOCTURNAL ANIMAL'S EYES?	
Yes, there are many rods in a nocturnal animal's eyes.	Some nocturnal animals have a few cones in their eyes. Others have no cones at all.

Rods and cones were named for their shapes.

MIRROR, MIRROR IN THE EYE

Cats also have a mirrorlike **layer** behind the retina called the tapetum lucidum. The tapetum lucidum **reflects** light back through the retina a second time, so the rods have another chance to collect it. When you shine a light into a cat's eyes at night, they appear to glow. The glow is the light reflected by the tapetum lucidum.

Not every nocturnal animal has the same color of glowing eyes. Cats' eyes shine green, while deer and raccoons' eyes are more yellow when they glow. Foxes' eyes usually shine white when they're caught in car headlights at night.

THAT MAKES SENSE!

Sometimes in a photo, a person's eyes look red. That's because their eyes are reflecting the camera flash back through the retina. The red color comes from the blood in the retina.

Have you ever seen a cat's eyes glow in the dark?

Here Comes the Sun

Because cats' eyes are so good at catching light in the darkness, they're **sensitive** to bright light. That's one reason why nocturnal animals aren't very active during the day. However, some nocturnal animals, such as house cats, are awake during the day. How do they see without hurting their eyes?

Humans have round pupils, which are great for daytime vision, but aren't very good at keeping light out. Cats and other nocturnal animals have slit pupils. Special muscles work like sliding doors to close the pupil quickly and keep the bright light out of a cat's eye, except for a tiny strip of light.

THAT MAKES SENSE!

Slit pupils can look different. They can look like horizontal lines, which go from side to side; vertical lines, which go up and down; or diagonal lines, which lean at an angle.

The shape of a person's pupils and a cat's pupils in bright light are very different.

WHO ELSE CAN SEE IN THE DARK?

Cats see better at night than most **mammals**, including humans. Owls have better night vision than most other birds. What other animals see well in the dark?

The tarsier is a small mammal that lives in southeastern Asia. Tarsiers are nocturnal animals with huge eyes that take in as much light as possible at night. In fact, they have the largest eyes of any mammal in **proportion** to their size. Like owls, tarsiers' eyes can't move in their sockets, but their neck turns their head much farther than many other animals.

THAT MAKES SENSE!

The giant leaf-tailed gecko also has huge eyes. It uses these huge eyes to see 350 times better in the dark than people can!

giant leaf-tailed gecko

tarsier

Both tarsiers and giant leaf-tailed geckos are known for their large eyes, which help these nocturnal animals find food and stay away from predators in the dark.

UNDERWATER AND IN THE AIR

Some animals live in ocean water so deep that sunlight can't reach them. One of these animals is the giant squid. It has eyes the size of dinner plates! These large eyes help it see its prey in dark ocean waters.

The spookfish is a fish that lives deep in the ocean. Scientists once thought it had four eyes. Now they know spookfish have two eyes split into halves. One half looks up, and the other half looks down into the dark. It also has mirrors in its eyes instead of lenses to aim light onto the retina.

THAT MAKES SENSE!

Giant squids have the largest eyes of any known animal on Earth.

giant squid

eye

Some bugs are also known for their strong sense of sight. A dragonfly is one of these bugs. Its eyes cover nearly its whole head!

Turn Off the Lights!

Sometimes, the things people build light up the darkness all night long, creating a problem called **light pollution**. This can be **dangerous** for nocturnal animals. They can't hide from predators. Their eyes are made for seeing in the dark and are sensitive to even tiny amounts of light, which can confuse them. They may stay away from areas where they've always lived in order to get away from the light.

Even the smallest change in surroundings can affect animals. If they move to an unfamiliar place to get away from bright lights, they may not know where to get food, have their babies, or hide from predators.

Oil rigs are built in the ocean, where they're used to drill for oil. They shine bright lights all night long and can be harmful to sea creatures with sensitive night vision.

21

SUPERIOR SIGHT

The changes that light pollution brings to an area are harmful to nocturnal animals. People can help by making sure their outside lights are off at night.

Cats have some cool abilities. They're great hunters, they can balance themselves almost anywhere, and they have excellent senses of smell and hearing. However, their most superior sense is their sense of sight. The next time you see your cat's eyes shine in the darkness, remember, that's how it can see you!

GLOSSARY

adapt: To change to fit new conditions.

dangerous: Not safe.

layer: One thickness of something lying over or under another.

light pollution: Light made by cities or buildings that gets in the way of natural light.

mammal: Any warm-blooded animal whose babies drink milk and whose body is covered with hair or fur.

muscle: A part of the body that produces motion.

prey: An animal hunted by other animals for food.

proportion: The relation of one part to another or to the whole.

reflect: To throw back light, heat, or sound.

sensitive: Easily hurt or damaged by an outside source.

socket: A hollow part in a bone that holds something else.

INDEX

WEBSITES

Due to the changing nature of Internet links, PowerKids Press has developed an online list of websites related to the subject of this book. This site is updated regularly. Please use this link to access the list: www.powerkidslinks.com/sas/cats